My First Book about the Alphabet of Primates

Amazing Animal Books Children's Picture Books

By Molly Davidson

Mendon Cottage Books

JD-Biz Publishing

Download Free Books!
http://MendonCottageBooks.com

All Rights Reserved.

No part of this publication may be reproduced in any form or by any means, including scanning, photocopying, or otherwise without prior written permission from JD-Biz Corp and http://AmazingAnimalBooks.com.
Copyright © 2016

All Images Licensed by Fotolia, Pixabay, and 123RF

Read More Amazing Animal Books

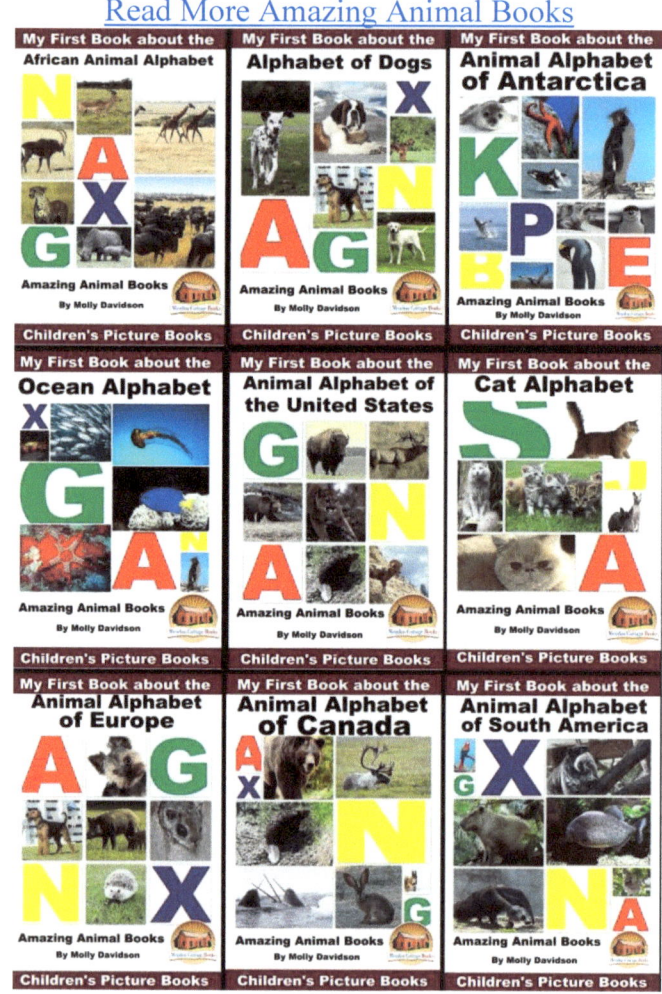

Purchase at Amazon.com

Download Free Books!

http://MendonCottageBooks.com

Introduction

Most primates use their fingers and toes very skillfully, which is very helpful as they climb, eat, and live in trees.

Most primates live in groups, called troops.

 is for an Aye-Aye.

nomis-simon © <u>Wikimedia Commons</u>

Aye-aye is a species of nocturnal lemur that lives in Madagascar and is endangered.

They have teeth that never stop growing, and eat seeds, fruit, flower nectar, and. grubs.

B is for a Baboon.

Baboons have lived in Africa for more than 2 million years.

Most baboons have a hairless pad on their bum, which makes sitting more comfortable.

B is also for a Bushbaby.

Bushbabies are nocturnal, active at night, and the most common primates in Africa.

The mothers usually give birth to twins during the rainy season.

They are related to lemurs and are very quick at jumping from tree to tree in the forest.

C  is for a Chimpanzee.

Chimpanzees live in groups of up to 150, but usually go looking for food in smaller groups.

They live to be about 50 years old.

 **is for a Douc.**

Douc live in family groups in the high forests
of Southeast Asia.

 **is for an Eastern Gorilla.**

Eastern gorillas are the largest living primates; some boys weigh up to 450 pounds and stand 5 1/2 feet tall.

Mothers have one baby about every 4 years.

The men defend the women and babies by beating their chests and charging any predators.

F is for a Formosan Rock Macaque.

© Wikimedia Commons

Formosan rock macaques are the only primates that live in Taiwan.

Mothers will carry their babies in their arms for the first 2 - 3 months, but the babies stay with their mother until they are about one year old.

G is for a Guenon.

Guenons are endangered and live in the sub-Saharan forests of Africa.

Hundreds of years ago some guenon were taken as pets by slaves, and traveled over the Atlantic and Caribbean Oceans, now a few live in the West Indian islands and Florida.

H is for a Howler.

Howler monkeys get their name from their loud howls, which can be heard 3 miles away, even in the thick South American forests.

They eat leaves, fruit, nuts, and flowers that grow at the top of the trees.

I is for an Indochinese Black Langur.

Robertpollai © **Wikimedia Commons**

The Indochinese black langur lives in Vietnam and Laos.

They eat mostly leaves, and a few fruits, seeds, flowers, and insects.

is for a Javan Lutung.

Javan lutung live on the island of Java in Indonesia and have very long tails, some over 3 feet in length.

 **is for a Kipunji.**

Zina Deretsky © <u>Wikimedia Commons</u>

Kipunji, also called the Highland Mangabey, lives high in the trees in Tanzania, Africa.

They are critically endangered, all the kipunji left live in just 7 square miles.

L is for a Lucifer Titi.

Greentrek Sustainable Travel © Wikimedia Commons

Lucifer titis live in South America in a family group of 2 - 7 members.

The father takes care of the baby, mothers are only in charge of feeding it milk when hungry.

 is for a Marmoset.

Marmosets live in the tropical forests of Brazil.

Babies take about 5 months to be born, and they are born usually as a twin.

They live in groups of up to 15.

 **is for a Night Monkey.**

Night monkeys, also called owl monkeys, live in Panama, and are the only monkey species to be nocturnal.

 is for an Orangutan.

Orangutans are a species of the great ape, and can only been found living in the rainforests of Borneo and Sumatra in Asia.

They are a very smart primate, and make very complicated nets from branches and leaves which they sleep in at night.

P is for a Pygmy Slow Loris.

Pygmy slow lorises live in the forests along the Mekong River in Asia.

They cannot jump from branch to branch; instead they crawl slowly up branches in search of prey.

 is for a Ring-Tailed Lemur.

Ring-tailed lemurs are endangered and can only be found living in Madagascar.

Their striped tails can be as long as 1 1/2 times their body length.

In the morning, they will sit up with their bellies facing the sun to get warm.

S is for a Spider Monkey.

Spider monkeys are an endangered species which live in the tropical forests of Central and South America.

They are very athletic and jump from tree to tree in the forest.

T is for a Tarsier.

Tarsiers live on the islands in Southeast Asia.

Each eye ball is 16 mm wide, which is bigger than their brain.

 **is for an Uakari.**

Uakari live in the tropical forests of South America in groups of up to 100.

They can leap over 18 feet!

V

is for a Vervet Monkey.

Vervet monkeys live mostly in Africa.

Their body is between 16 - 20 inches long.

They have up to 30 different alarm calls which they use to warn each other of danger.

W  is for a Woolly Monkey.

Woolly monkeys live in the Rainforests of South America, high in the trees.

They use their long tails to grab and hold on to branches so they can eat with both hands.

X is for S. Xanthosternos, the scientific name for a Golden-Bellied Capuchin.

Golden-bellied capuchins are critically endangered and are only found in the Atlantic Forest in Bahia, Brazil.

 **is for a Yellow-Cheeked Gibbon.**

Yellow-cheeked gibbons are another endangered primate, which live in the tropical forests of Vietnam, Laos, and Cambodia.

Gibbons will sing together to show that they are a couple and are bonding.

 **is for a Zanzibar Red Colobus.**

Zanzibar red colobuses are endangered and are only found on the Zanzibar Archipelago off the coast of Tanzania, Africa.

Conclusion

I hope you have enjoyed this book about the amazing anima called the primate.

One more fact, chimpanzees are the closets living relative to humans, 99% of their DNA is common to a humans.

Download Free Books!

http://MendonCottageBooks.com

Purchase at Amazon.com
Website http://AmazingAnimalBooks.com

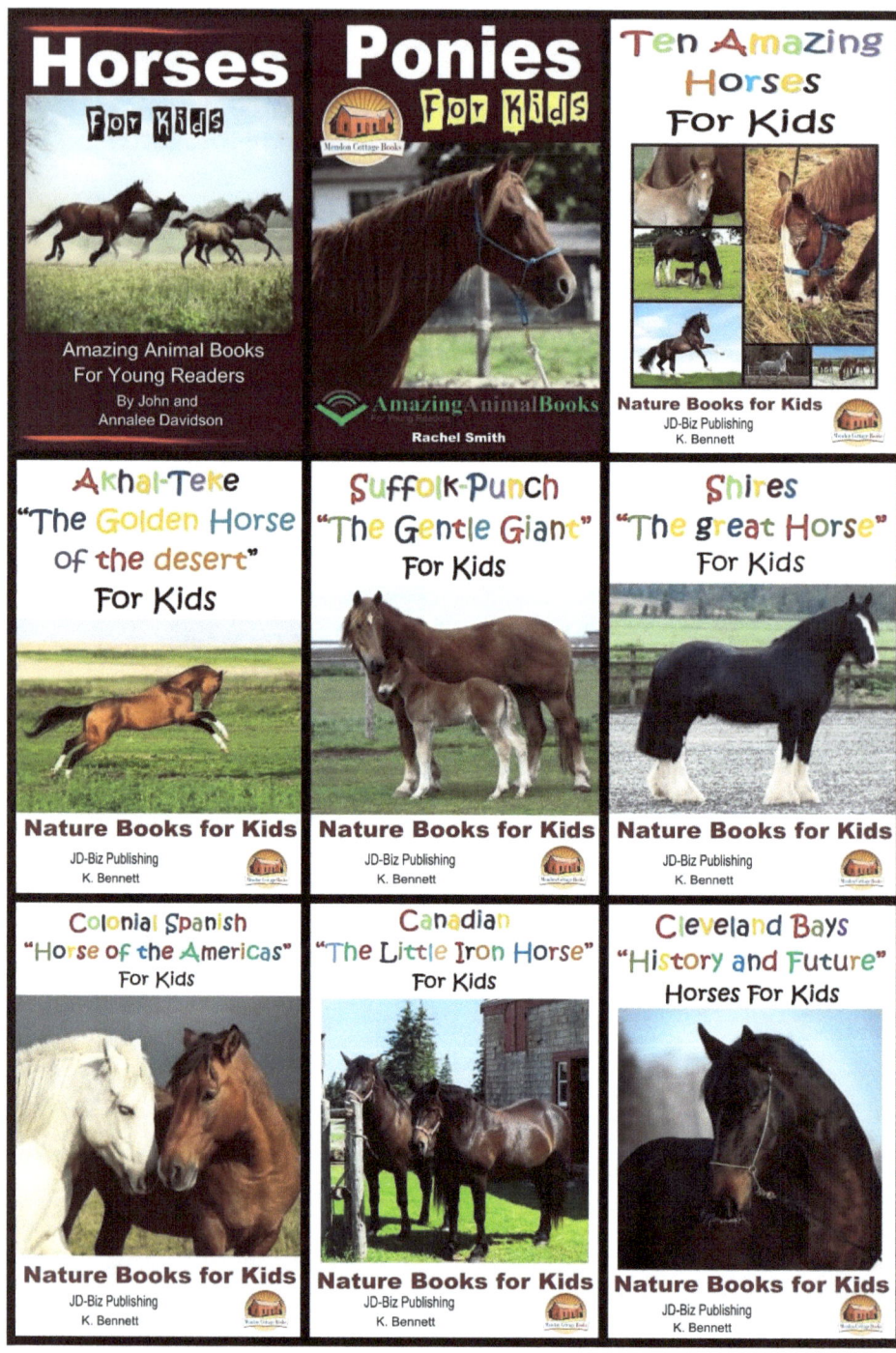

Our books are available at

1. Amazon.com

2. Barnes and Noble

3. Itunes

4. Kobo

5. Smashwords

6. Google Play Books

Download Free Books!
http://MendonCottageBooks.com

Publisher

JD-Biz Corp

P O Box 374

Mendon, Utah 84325

http://www.jd-biz.com/

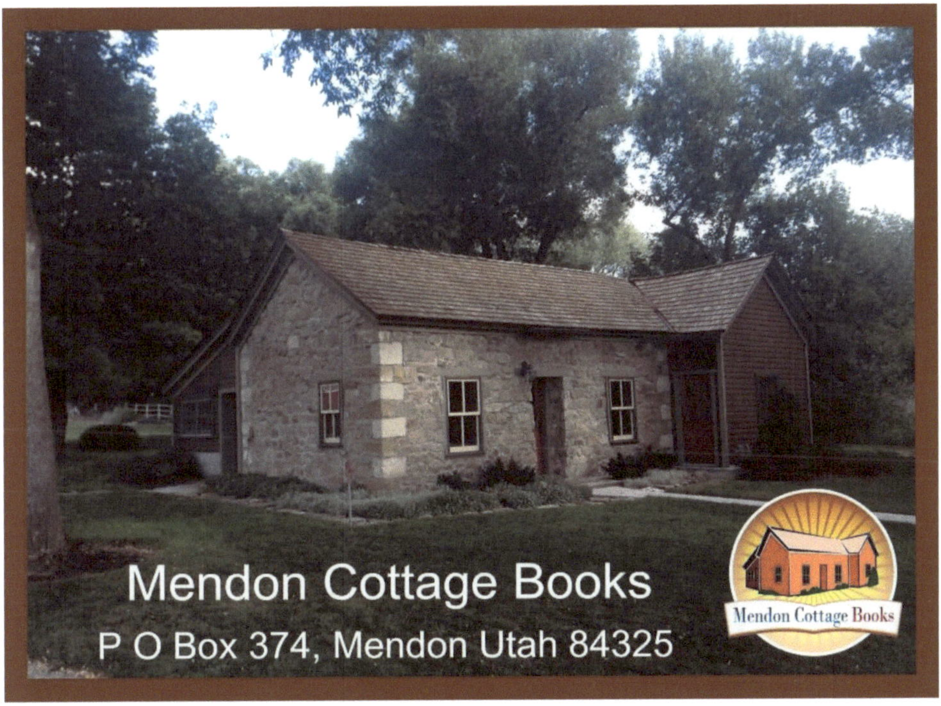

![Mendon Cottage Books, P O Box 374, Mendon Utah 84325]

www.ingramcontent.com/pod-product-compliance
Lightning Source LLC
Chambersburg PA
CBHW050903290526
45792CB00002B/678